# ADOBE
## Remodeling & Fireplaces

# ADOBE
## Remodeling & Fireplaces

Myrtle Stedman

Sunstone Press
Santa Fe, New Mexico

*To my grandchildren, Marilyn, Kathleen,*
*Robin, Denise, Ward and Paul.*

I wish to pay homage to those who have encouraged my work in adobe design and building leading to this publication: First, to Wilfred Stedman, my husband, whose knowledge and love of adobe brought me to it as well and made all things possible; to J.R. Chillman, former head of the Department of Architecture at Rice Institute and curator of the Houston Art Museum; to Robert Brown, Grace Spaulding John, Beulah Ayers, Robert Henri, John F. Carlson and Ward Lockwood, artists. To Willard Kruger, Kenneth Clark and Truman Mathews, architects; F.A. Berry, President of the Big Jo Lumber Company of Santa Fe, New Mexico; Oliver LaFarge, Southwestern writer; Randall Davey, painter; W.M. Williams when he was a Vice President of B.B.D. & O., Advertising Agency; C.C. Bennett, executive in the publication department of the *Sweet's Catalog;* Irene Peck, Director of the New Mexico State Library Extension Service which eventually became the New Mexico State Library; the Caprons of Pojoaque; to Jody Ellis and Marcia Muth of the *Sunstone Press* and to all the Spanish-speaking people and Indians who worked at one time or another for me or for "The Tesuque Home Builders." These have been the related and unrelated Griegos; Demacio, Anistacio, Redolfo, Juan and Ramon Griego. There were the Conchas of the Taos Pueblo, John D. and Eva, his wife; his son Delfino, and his brother Nick; and Redolfinio Gonzales of Tesuque, all expert in adobe or carpentry; and many others who were their helpers — to all, my appreciation and my thanks. And thanks to Mr. and Mrs. Arturo Jaramillo for letting me use a nice old panel-faced fireplace design from their Rancho de Chimayo Restaurant in *Adobe Remodeling.*

Printed in the United States of America

10 9 8 7 6 5 4 3

Library of Congress Cataloging in Publication Data:

Stedman, Myrtle.
Adobe: remodeling & fireplaces.

Bibliography: p. 44.
Includes index.
1. Adobe houses--Remodeling. 2. Building, Adobe.
3. Fireplaces--Design and construction. I. Title.
TH4818.A3S744    1986    693'.22    86-5744
ISBN: 0-86534-086-2

Published by SUNSTONE PRESS
Post Office Box 2321
Santa Fe, NM 87504-2321 / USA
(505) 988-4418 / *orders only* (800) 243-5644
FAX (505) 988-1025

# CONTENTS

Remodeling of Adobe **7**
Adobe Fireplaces **35**
Bibliography **44**
Index **45**

# REMODELING OF ADOBE

Adobe (earth mixed with straw and water) lends itself beautifully to architectural form and to the remodeling of form. In arid areas such as Santa Fe and surrounding villages and towns where adobe is readily available and climatic conditions favor its use, we need not think of an adobe building as an absolute entity that can neither be added to nor taken from. Traditionally, the history of an adobe house starts with four walls, a fireplace and a roof overhead; the structure is referred to simply as "an adobe," though it may grow to house four generations or generation upon generation, a congregation, a state or local business. The lasting qualities of the old adobes can only be attributed to the massive preponderance of adobe used in both outside and inside wall structure which presents a homogeneous self-supporting unit. For the past thirty years, because of labor costs, and a certain lack of appreciation for adobe a lot of frame and block have been used partially or in complete substitution for adobe. Now there is an upsurge of interest in adobe and in the art and science of designing and building in adobe. Remodeling an old house built solidly of adobe can be very rewarding in retaining the soft acoustical nature of its structure as well as in maintaining coolness in the summer, warmth in the winter, and in preserving the many other charming qualities for which a real adobe is known.

# ADDING TO
# AND REMODELING AN
# OLD ADOBE

The drawings on this page are a reprint from page 4 of our book *Adobe Architecture.* They show a Pueblo-style adobe house designed for a small family. Let us say that it was built directly from this book in 1936 when the book was first published. By now, if the same family is living in it, their children have grown up and moved away but return occasionally to visit, bringing with them their own children. Let us say that the location is ideal and that the home has greater possibilities than have ever been realized. Let us imagine that the living room windows look onto a small hill covered with tumbleweed, whereas a living room on the other side of the house could have a beautiful mountain view, and a view up and down a river with cottonwoods along its banks. The father is retired. His hobby is music and Aunt Mary has just left him a grand piano. An accumulation of books has been crowding the small house.

SO LET US BUILD A NEW LIVING ROOM-LIBRARY combination into one generous-sized room; build a new master bedroom and bath off that; then remodel the old part.

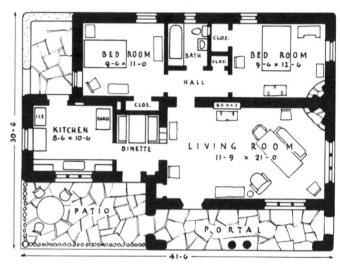

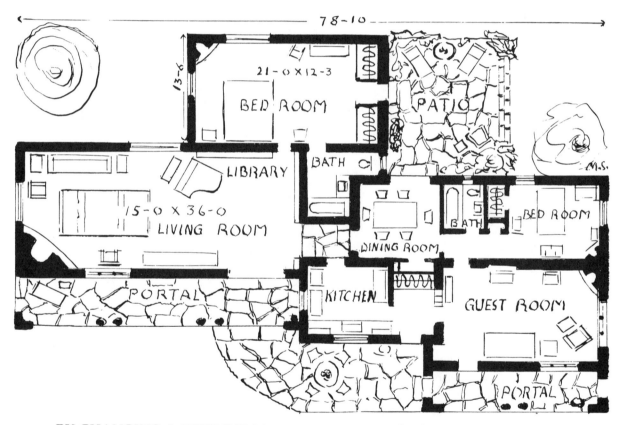

BY CHANGING A BEDROOM into a much-needed dining room we can turn the original dinette area into a closet off the existing living room. The old living room could then become a dorm for the visiting grandchildren; or it could be a TV room, a sewing room or just a fun room.

THE NEW ARRANGEMENT LOOKS excellent on paper, showing the advantages of a free flow of traffic and a new feeling of openness in all directions. The house can be doubled in size and remodeled in a little more than half the time it would take to build a new house, and usually life can go practically undisturbed in the old part until the new part is ready to move into.

## BOND BETWEEN THE NEW AND THE OLD

NEW CONSTRUCTION will not be discussed here except to say that unless otherwise desired there should be a bond between the new and the old in design as well as in structure. New innovations should blend with the old or the old should be brought up to date to match the new. Physically the new framing and new adobe walls should dovetail into the old so that there is no pulling away or leaning in or out.

DOVETAILING SHOULD START WITH THE FOUNDATION by beginning the new foundation *under* the old foundation where the walls are to abut one another, or by starting the new foundation *against* the old in a short T-shape. All dirt should be cleaned away from the old foundation so that the new cement will bond to the old cement.

WALL DOVETAILING can be accomplished by digging into the old wall at intervals so that a brick of the new wall can extend a couple of inches into the old wall. New window lintels or beams extending into old walls are also a great help in tying the new to the old.

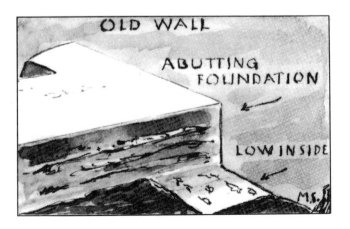

OVERLAPPING ROOFS. In this plan none of the old copings need to be disturbed. The roofing on the new part can be carried up over the old copings. Vigas for the new bath and hall can take the same direction as the living room vigas as they can be carried into the end wall of the kitchen. One viga should go against the old wall to support the ends of the ceiling boards.

THE NEW BATH is located conveniently close to the old bath and to the kitchen so that water and sewage shouldn't be too much of a problem.

ELECTRICAL EXPANSION will call for updating circuit breakers and fuse boxes.

THE ARCHITECTURAL DESIGN of the new portal uses the same double-post grouping and double-corbel headings as the present portal. The same is true of the adobe corner supports. The two portals will appear almost as one and will be linked together with a curved flagstone walk.

HEATING will need to be extended or perhaps the whole system restudied for a decision as to how this should be handled.

THE INTERIOR DESIGN can show the same deep window reveals (the vertical sides of the opening in the wall, from edge to window frame). It can also show the same wall treatment on walls and fireplace, and matching woodwork — or at least enough of the same so that the new and the old will carry out the same architectural style.

## NEW OPENINGS
## IN OLD WALLS

Structurally there are only three changes to be made in the old part of the house to comply with the new arrangement. They involve making a closet in the end of the old dinette area, the removal of two windows in the old bedroom which is to be the new dining room, and the installation of doors in place of the windows.

UNDER AN OLD WINDOW LINTEL a door can be hung on a new frame with no problem, after the old window frame and window are removed and the adobes cleanly cut out, down to the floor. This we can take advantage of where one window is to become the doorway to the new living room.

IN THE WEIGHT-BEARING WALL the removal of the other window and the installation of the sliding glass door which will open onto the flagged area is more complicated. Vigas rest on this wall, carrying part of the weight of ceiling and roof, and the space we want to open is wide. Dotted lines on the wall (see center drawing) show what the width of the opening is to be. We can locate the opening so that the total weight of only two

vigas and their ceiling load will be on the lintel over the opening after it is made, and we can support at least these two vigas by upright posts so that we can channel the wall for the new lintel and for the removal of the existing short lintel. The new lintel will consist of two full-length timbers cut two feet longer than the width of the proposed opening. By using two timbers for the new lintel, one timber can be put in from the inside while half of the wall remains in place until this timber is fitted into place and ready to carry its half of the load. Then the lintel can be completed by putting the other timber in from the outside of the building. This second timber should be fitted in tightly so that both are ready to carry the load.

THE SUPPORT POSTS can then be removed and the opening safely made for the sliding glass door. This same method can be used for putting in a large window in a weight-bearing wall.

NEW OPENINGS IN A NON-WEIGHT-BEARING WALL can be made by putting in the lintel in two sections or timbers as described above, but no props should be necessary. There is a paragraph about lintels in *Adobe Architecture* (p. 33)

which may be helpful.

REMOVING ADOBES FROM AN OLD WALL is not difficult. The whole ones can be separated easily one by one when a flat shovel, a trowel, or a leaf of an old car spring is used to pry them apart at their joints. For cutting in a straight downward line, several strands of barbed wire twisted together with loops at the ends and used in the manner of a cross-cut saw can't be equaled. The whole adobes and sound pieces can be saved and used again.

NAILING BLOCKS should first be put in and allowed to set before window or door frames are to be installed. See *Adobe Architecture,* pp. 32 and 33.

## MENDING ADOBE PLASTER

Assuming that the wall in this room where the window and door changes have been made was plastered with adobe, the patching would be made with adobe plaster. The first coat would have fine straw mixed into it, the second coat no straw. Areas to be plastered should first be cleaned of all loose adobe and protrusions. Nailing blocks and lintel ends should have metal lath nailed to them. The areas to be plastered should be sprinkled with water from a brush dipped in a pail of water; then the patch plaster-

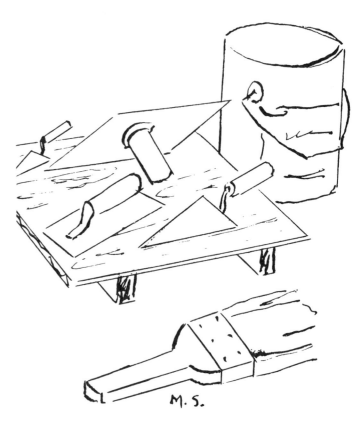

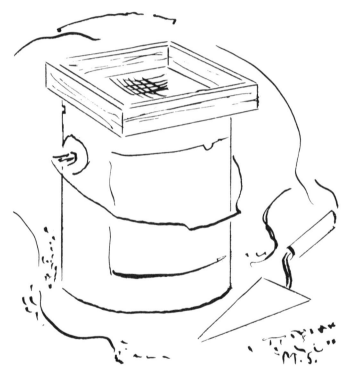

ing should begin by tightly filling in between frame and wall and over metal lath. This should finish roughly $1/8$ of an inch below the surface of the undisturbed plaster, and be allowed plenty of time to dry thoroughly before the second coat is applied. The second coat of plaster should be of a finer texture, the dry contents having been put through a finer screen before water was added. After the second coat is put on and has set slightly, it can be smoothed down flush with the adjoining wall until all trace of rough edges of the patch are removed. A plasterer's float, a piece of sheep's skin, or a damp kitchen sponge can be used for this. The patched area should be finished like the original plaster so that the texture of both is the same.

ADOBE FOR PLASTERING is the same as for adobes or mortar, except it is put through a finer screen. It is a right combination of clay and sand mixed in a workable proportion of each. It should have no humus, so is usually found in a more or less barren place, probably in our own back yard. Testing can be made in a trial patch of plaster. If it cracks badly, more sand should be added to the mix. If it crumbles when dry, it needs more clay. Too much water washes out the adhesive quality of the clay. Experience is the best teacher. Properly mixed, the adobe will slip cleanly from the trowel and not pull or roll under it.

SCREENS are kept by people who habitually or periodically patch adobe. They are usually made of 2 x 4 lumber and screening which may be either full-width and four or five feet long; or small enough to fit over a wheel-barrow or even a bucket. The screening may be of various sizes of mesh — $1/4$ inch for material for first coats, $1/8$ inch or fly screen for the finish. The dry adobe and sand are passed separately through the screens onto a clean surface into two separate piles until ready to be used.

MENDING HARD PLASTER. If the walls of the house being remodeled have hard plaster over adobe, the spaces between adobe and new frames or any other large break can be filled in with adobe first. Chicken wire or metal lath must be nailed over the adobe to hold the hard plaster. The same techniques as in adobe plastering are those used to apply a fibered first coat, then a finish plaster second coat. Small cracks or nail holes in a hard-plastered wall may be filled with Spackling Compound or with a plaster made of Dry Latex Cement, then smoothed with a damp piece of sheepskin before it dries so that the patch will not show when it is painted.

ALL PLASTER, adobe or hard, should be cleaned from woodwork before it has time to set; otherwise it will stain the woodwork.

PAINTING of newly plastered walls should not be done before a sealer or protective coat is used to prevent scalding (chemical discoloration).

AN OLD CUSTOM OF PAINTING adobe walls is to paint a one-inch strip of paint onto the ceiling and around vigas or beams. It is much easier and gives the authentic look to a new paint job. When this is done, the walls and ceiling curve softly together instead of coming against each other in a sharp, harsh line. Also, particularly in the old Pueblo-style houses, it is very common to see a darker harmonizing color toward the base of the room and around doors and windows. This practice had its practical purpose also, but established a very decorative effect. Sometimes a symbolical design was painted over this base color.

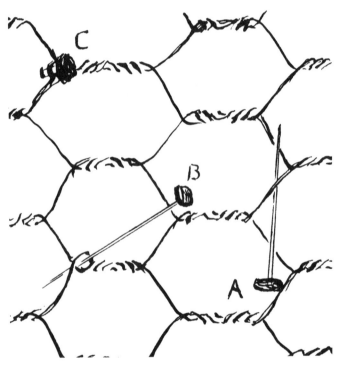

16

OIL OR WATER COLOR PAINT-INGS can be hung from a nail driven into adobe walls if there is no electrical wiring buried in the area. There is also a metal strip designed to be nailed to the wall about eye level before plastering is done. Only a horizontal valley is seen after the plastering and painting is completed. The paintings are to hang from this valley.

HEAVY MIRRORS, CABINETS, HANGING SHELVES of the kind so often seen in adobe houses can be successfully hung from a spike driven into the adobe wall at a slightly downward angle with carefully measured short strokes of the hammer, or from an anchor which works on the expansion principle, made especially to be used in an adobe wall. A slender three to three-and-a-half inch long cement coated nail should be sufficient for hanging lighter weight things. A nail shorter than two inches will hardly hold anything, whereas a huge spike is seldom necessary.

Other problems that might have come up in this particular remodeling job may be handled later.

WILFRED STEDMAN

## REMOVING A NON-WEIGHT BEARING WALL

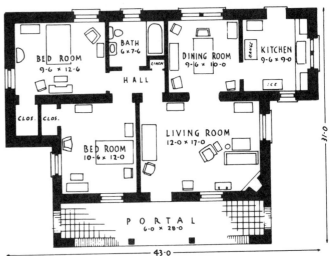

To illustrate how simple this could be, the Spanish-Colonial house on page 15 of *Adobe Architecture* was chosen. If the people who have such a house rarely need space for overnight guests but do entertain frequently, they may want to take the partition wall out between the bedroom and the living room and devote all this floor space to the living room, as shown in the plan on the opposite page. If we had shown the complete plan for the original building we would have shown the beams in both rooms running from back to front and matching in size and character and probably would have shown the same ceiling structure. These are the first things to check for. Next, one should check to see if there is a beam where the partition is, or if one will have to be put in. If this is an older house or as we would have designed it, this part of the house would have been originally built as one room and the beam would be there. The partition wall would have no structural significance except to divide the area into two rooms. Ideally, the flooring will match and not be difficult to fill in. If these conditions obtain it would be a simple matter to remove the par-

W.S.

tition wall which is shown in this plan as a stud wall with plaster board and plaster. If things are not all this simple, with imagination and proper engineering it can still be done.

SEALING UP THE DOORWAYS on the living room side that lead to the hall, would give the owners a chance to arrange the living room more comfortably, while making the bath and remaining bedroom more private from the entertainment area.

SHELVES FOR BOOKS AND KNICKKNACKS can be put in the door frames on the hall-way side, which will show from the dining room, since opening a new door from the dining room to the hall-way would be imperative.

THE PEOPLE AND THEIR FRIENDS could be delighted with the spacious feeling that would take place in this small homelike high country dwelling. If the joys of having a larger living room outweigh the advantages which having an extra bedroom once had, then removing this wall would be a huge success.

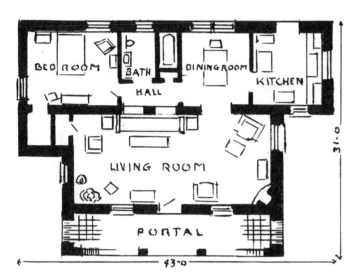

# REMOVING PART OF A WEIGHT-BEARING WALL

The Old Mexico style house reproduced from page 20 of *Adobe Architecture* presents two possibilities for removing part of weight-bearing wall. With a wider doorway we could open up the kitchen area into the enclosed patio. The wall here would be carrying part of the weight of both the kitchen and the patio ceilings by having beams from both these areas resting on it. To do this we would duplicate the method of propping the vigas shown on page 12 of this book, while putting in a longer heavier lintel in the same manner in which the one of the sliding glass door was installed. And the same thing could be done between the living room and the dining room.

IT WOULD NOT BE WISE to remove the whole wall between these two rooms. In both cases an opening just twice the width of the present doorways would greatly increase the feeling of openness, and again create a feeling of space in a small house. The dining room would then be more accessible to the living room for buffet type of entertaining, and the patio would be more fun by being directly connected to the area where food is

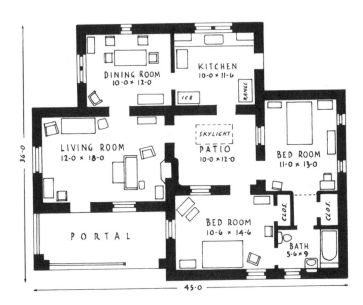

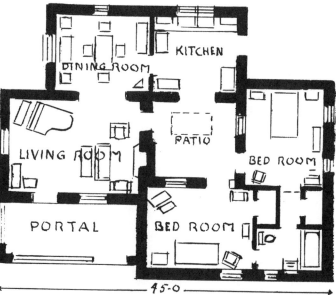

prepared. Moreover, both kitchen and patio would share increased light and greenery.

THE WEIGHT TO BE PASSED ON DOWN to the new lintel should never be under-estimated. The lintel timbers should be used on edge to utilize the full strength of their depth to prevent sagging, and their extension into the wall on both sides of the opening should be sufficient to give good shouldering for this weight (10 to 12 inches).

ROOF STRAIN AND CRACKING OF ROOF MATERIAL may take place if care is not taken in using the props while doing this work on a Pueblo-style house with flat roof. Props must support the weight but not force the vigas out of place. If cracks appear on a flat roof, the proper method of repair should be employed. When the roofing paper in the area is cleaned of all dirt, dust, and loose gravel, a swath of Plastic Cement can be spread over the crack, extending several inches on both sides of it. A width of roofing cloth wide enough to cover the cemented area should then be laid over it and cemented down. The process should be repeated until two or three layers are covering the area. The dirt and gravel can then be put back over the mend to protect the roof from sun and hail. As soon as the props are down, this roof checking and repair should be done so that a sudden rain will not wash out the work just done inside.

A MEXICAN TILE PITCHED ROOF over a flat ceiling, as shown here in this Old Mexico house, does not present the problem a flat-roofed Pueblo-style house would.

## RESTORING A RUIN

A ruin is usually a ruin because the roof is entirely or partially gone, or because surface water has done its damage in some areas near the foundation. But if there is enough sound wall structure, these conditions may be remedied without tearing down completely and beginning all over again. Some thick-walled adobe ruins have possibilities of charm that could never be attained in a new structure.

FIREPLACES may be one of the most fascinating things about an old adobe, but should be carefully inspected for deterioration at the ceiling and roof levels before any fires are lighted. Many chimneys were built without clay flue linings. If there are signs of smoke on the ceiling or vigas near the chimney as though the smoke came from that area and not from the fireplace itself, it is certain the chimney should be torn down below that level and rebuilt. Sometimes charred ceiling boards are not discovered until the chimney is torn down. Rebuilding the chimney can make the fireplace safe again.

ROOF DAMAGE usually occurs where canales have been allowed to deteriorate. The viga may be rotted away at such places and the wall

eroded. Or leakage around the coping may affect other viga ends where they rest on the wall. Too, the whole upper part of the walls may be in so crumbling a condition that they must come out as far down as window openings; yet, they are worth doing. One hopes only canales, copings, and eroded areas will need to be rebuilt and the roofing repaired or done over. A flat-roofed house will need a new roof job about every twenty years. Canales and the upturn to copings because of their extreme exposure to expansion and contraction from changing temperatures, need to be checked yearly for breaks and mended if necessary, with Plastic Cement and roofing cloth. Many old buildings have heavy, well-seasoned and beautifully patina'd beams and ceilings which for the most part may be perfectly sound. It is possible to cut away the rotted ends of one or two beams, splice them with new material, and avoid the complete replacement of ceiling and roof by building in an ingenious closet, bookcase, or partial wall to give these support, if necessary. Or a corbel, built into the wall under a spliced beam or viga end may suffice. If a viga needs to be completely removed and replaced, it can be cut and carefully pulled away from the ceiling and down into the room. A new viga may then be threaded through the hole in the wall from the outside and across under the ceiling and up into the hole in the far wall, where wedges

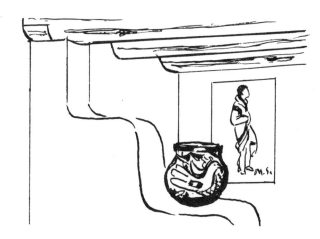

Coping

Canale

Splice

Old Viga

Corbel

Outside

Wall

Inside

Cross-sectional Drawing

M.S.

and adobes will press it against the ceiling. The ceiling boards can then be nailed to it and the roof patched in that spot. If complete replacement of ceiling and roof is necessary, sound parts of the old material may be re-used in new contruction to obtain beautiful results.

A BEAM CRACKED CROSS-WAYS is no longer sound as a full-length beam but it can be cut into two usable pieces. A beam cracked length-wise, because of uneven drying in seasoning, may be perfectly sound for its total length. It is neither uncom-mon nor unpleasant to see these cracks in a beam. Old lumber should not be discarded simply because it is old. It may be tough from seasoning, and a more generous cut than a new piece. Its scars can be treated and coaxed into real beauty.

CRACKS IN THE WALL OF A RUIN resulting from an undermined foun-dation are indications that the foun-dation should be reenforced by pour-ing a new reenforced section underneath the weakened area. After the cause has been corrected, if the crack has occurred where a door or window is to be cut and installed in the wall, the new lintel may bridge the gap, stitching the wall together. If the wall is to remain solid a buttress against the wall on the outside may be a colorful solution. A crack in a weight-bearing wall deserves more at-tention than if it were in an end wall. We are not concerned with surface cracks but with the ones which go all the way through the wall. A new coat of plaster will eventually take care of the mended wall cracks and the small cracks.

FOUNDATION REENFORCEMENT for ruins constructed before the days of cement foundations should be made to keep moisture from coming through to the base of the house. Where the walls seem solid it can be assumed that the rock and adobe foundations will still hold, but to help them to hold and to protect them

24

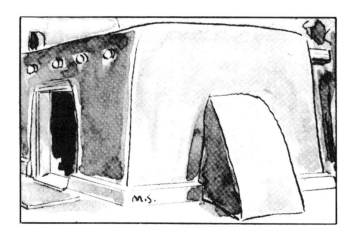

from further erosion from surface water, a narrow cement foundation reenforcement may be run along the outside of the old foundation. The trench for this should be dug down to below frost level, and eroded and loose material cleaned from the rocks of the old foundation so that the new cement will interlace with it. Below ground level, the ground itself can serve as a form for cement and re-enforcing rods. Above ground level there should be forms so that the cement can be brought up tight to ten inches or more to finish with a beveled ledge so that melting snow and rain will run away from the walls instead of soaking into them. It is well to run such a protection all around the outside walls, a typical feature to be found in a well-cared-for old house. Buttresses have this distinction also. Because both the buttress and foundation reenforcement methods of repair are so frequent they each have become an integral feature of adobe architecture.

# FLOORS

Any type of floor having a cultural or historic value is fun to preserve or duplicate.

FLOORS OF ADOBE ARE THE VERY OLDEST type and still the most revered. In the simplest form the ground is leveled, swept, sprinkled, and tamped. In the more sophisticated floor the tamped earth is covered with about a one-inch layer of adobe and straw much like a first coat of plaster on an adobe wall. This is allowed to dry thoroughly and a finer second coat is troweled on the same as a second coat of plaster is put on. When the adobe floor is laid by women the adobe, straw and water are kneaded in a pan as they would knead bread dough. The kneading compresses the air and excess water out of the mixture and takes less time to dry than the plastering method. After the floor is dry, kneaded mix is rolled between the hands and the roll pressed into the cracks and smoothed with damp sheepskin. Then the whole floor is washed with a thin mix of adobe which has been selected for color, usually reddish-brown.

FOR A SURFACE HARDENER, ox-blood was used in the old days. That was superseded by the hardener used

26

today — a hot mixture of 2 parts of Boiled Linseed Oil to 1 part of turpentine for a first treatment; subsequent treatments of cold Boiled Linseed Oil are made two or three weeks apart and whenever the floor needs refreshing. Burnt sienna oil paint may be added to the first hot treatment to give the floor color if this method is preferred. When the oil is thoroughly dry the floor can be waxed, damp mopped and dusted with an oil mop as any other waxed floor.

Adobe floors seem to have a springy resilience. Very often these floors will be completely or partly-covered with handwoven rugs. Where the floors show they will be a mahogany brown with bits or streaks of straw glowing golden beneath the surface.

DAMAGE TO ADOBE FLOORS can be repaired by breaking away the loose portion and building up again. The oil treatment will blend the patched area into the old area so that it becomes unnoticable.

FLAGSTONE AND BRICK and other types of earth floors are sometimes laid directly on a base of loose adobe or sand, with cement used only in the joints. This can only be done in an arid climate where there is little danger from water. Care must be taken to keep surface water and dampness away from outside founda-

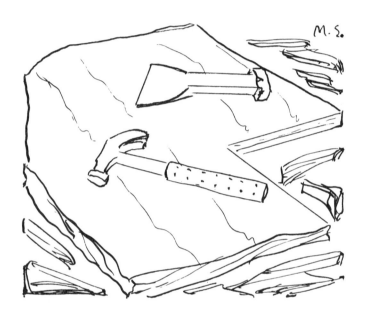

tions. Earthen flooring laid on earth conducts warmth from the earth itself, and high sills keep out drafts and blowing dust, so in this dry land we often find ourselves stepping down into an adobe house rather than up into one. But for standard practice a raised reenforced slab of concrete should form the base for flagstone or brick floors. The flagstone is brushed with a wet brush and placed wet side down in dry cement which has been lightly sprinkled over a small placement of fresh cement, about two inches thick on the slab. Bricks should be soaked and damp when laid. There should be about a half-inch space left between stones and brick for grouting, which is done after they have set. Dry cement can be cleaned from their surfaces with a dry burlap bag.

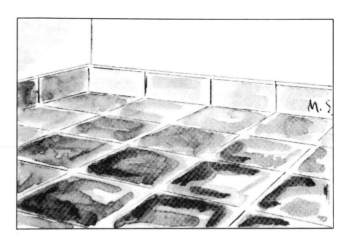

TOOLS FOR CUTTING FLAGSTONE and brick are a metal straight-edge for use in scoring, a stoneman's chisel, and an old hammer. For precision cutting a skilsaw with a masonry blade or a diamond blade and a water attachment for the saw is used.

TREATMENT OF FLAGSTONE AND BRICK floors can be the same as for an adobe floor: hot 2 parts of Boiled Linseed Oil to one part of

turpentine followed by cold applications of the Boiled Linseed Oil for a stain resistant waxable surface.

LARGE SQUARE FLOOR TILE is another clay product. This should be laid in mastic or in mortar on a cement slab. Cutting is done with an electric tile saw.

FLAGS OR PLAIN SQUARE TILE look good in a pueblo-style adobe. The square is an important Indian symbol, and flags are a natural.

BRICKS ARE USED MOSTLY in the Territorial Adobes. The use of brick and milled lumber created the style, when those materials were brought in over the newly opened Santa Fe Trail while New Mexico was a territory.

PLAIN SQUARE TILES are used in the Old Mexico style home, but are nice in any of our houses.

WOODEN PLANK FLOORS pegged to wooden joists may be found in an old adobe. If so, the knots will be shiny, the soft wood worn down around them and in paths, telling the story of generations of footsteps. These floors could be repaired, cleaned up and treated like an old piece of antique furniture, letting the high spots and worn paths give a grace and feeling of ease to the house. If setting has occurred, joist repair or support may be indicated. Such remodeling may be done for love rather than to save money, but if the floor is not too bad, remodeling may save money, too.

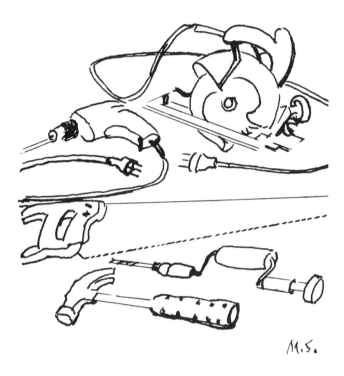

29

# WINDOWS

In the earliest adobes in the pueblos, windows were just peep holes. Even after mica and then glass came into use, windows were small and sparingly used. The north side of an adobe rarely had a window, even in the Spanish Colonial or Territorial days, and that is still true where the owner is concerned with keeping his house warm with very little heat. An adobe is a solid edifice against the elements, an environment all to itself with its fireplaces for companionship and ventilation.

MODERN BUILDING REQUIREMENTS call for a certain amount of light and ventilation in a room. More modern inventions call for keeping the windows closed. So just how much light and ventilation one needs, how much indoor outdoor feeling, or how much privacy one wants, are all questions one should ask before putting a lot of new windows in an old house.

ANY STANDARD TYPE OF WINDOW can be installed in an adobe. If there is enough masonry on either side of a window, a large window will not destroy the adobe look of solidarity, especially if smaller panes

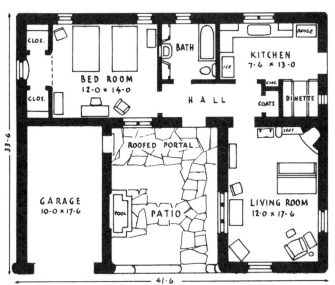

break up the glass area. The most characteristic thing about a window in an adobe house is the deep window reveal, either to the inside or to the outside, and the style in which it is framed.

## DOORS AND DOORWAYS

All of the distinctive architectural features of an adobe doorway are based on simple practicality, handled in a loving and beautiful way. Outside doorways are always raised slightly, as is the ground all around the house to carry sudden heavy rainfall away from the adobe. High sills provide protection to the inside of the house from water or the ravages of winds and ground storms. Further protection may be provided by an unroofed walled area which embraces a high-silled door before the main entrance. Typically, inside are high sills and steps up or down to differing floor levels.

THE WAY THE DOOR IS FRAMED AND HANGS is part of the picture also. Often a door from one room to another may swing on balls and sockets rather than hinges. The balls are a part of the door itself which fit into sockets bored into the lintel overhead, and into the sill. When side frames (jambs) first came into use

6 - 3

42"

B

C

$2\frac{1}{2}$" M.S.

$2\frac{1}{2}$"

DOUBLE DOORS

24"x6-8

M.S.

NEW SLABS AND OLD 1 x 4

32

they were notched into the head piece and into the sill, so that these two members were still integral parts of the frame. This type of door framing is very practical for an adobe house, causing little or no pull and strain on the walls in which they function. The side pieces are thick enough so that heavy doors hinged to them will not pull the frames out of place. On these doors the hardware is usually heavy hand-wrought iron in either simple or elaborate form, and the doors are of heavy hand-hewn or rough-sawn material. Lighter weight doors can take the lighter weight conventional framing.

Doors are usually morticed and tendoned in their joints and paneling. Mill shops specialize in making doors of this type, and they may be heavily carved to offset and enhance the adobe simplicity. Carving was a Spanish influence added to the Pueblo-style building. In the Territorial days of early 1900's a plank door held together with nailed or hand-routed molding enhanced the Territorial home.

TO MAKE THE TERRITORIAL DOOR no expensive equipment is needed. If a molding plane can not be found, commercial molding can be substituted with ingenuity. The planks should be cut to the desired width and height for the door: then they are laid side-by-side on a flat surface leveled with a level, otherwise a decided and permanent warp might be built in. The molding is nailed to the planks in such a way as to hold them together, to cover some if not all of the cracks, to give thickness, especially to the door edges, as well as to create a beautiful door. The square-cut nails should be long enough to go through molding and planks so they can be bent over on the other side of the door and act not only as nails but as clamps. The nails, wrought iron hinges, and lock will streak the planks with rust and afford the only decoration on the otherwise plain side of the door. Sometimes moldings are put on both sides of the planks, but this was rarely done in the old days.

DOUBLE DOORS were sometimes made for main entrances to the house or to the courtyard. When used for the courtyard, they often had a smaller door within one of the larger doors. Such double doors could also be used as garage doors.

A FINAL WORD: If you understand why things are the way they are in an old adobe house, appreciate what is there and make use of it — that is, if you understand the soul and spirit of adobe architecture — then you will experience a special joy in adobe remodeling. I toast those who have this unique experience!

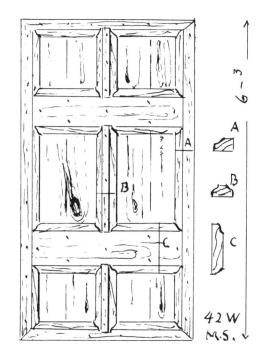

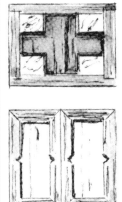

33

# ADOBE FIREPLACES

From the beginning of time, man, his family and friends have gathered around the fire for cooking purposes, for comfort and companionship. Even when not in use a fireplace is a focal point of interest and beauty in a home. In particular, fireplaces seem indigenous to adobe houses. In fact, no adobe house seems complete without one. It is the heart of the house radiating warmth enveloping all who enter. Or, for one alone, a fire in a fireplace is like a presence in the room of universal stature, inviting one to reminisce on all that is good and holy. It can be like a shrine in a home or companion to merrymaking and frolicking. It can be a place to put potatoes or carrots seasoned and buttered, wrapped in foil and buried in the ashes, or a marinated chuck roast to be cooked liked a steak on a grid over low coals. It can have bancos embracing it on either side or it can stand alone on its own merits.

In the illustrations of our book *Adobe Architecture,* we have shown twelve fireplaces. Though design possibilities are as infinite in adobe as in any other masonry material, the fundamental construction of the working elements of a fireplace can best be illustrated in the simplest and dearest to our hearts, the corner fireplace. This is so as the earliest of adobe fireplace builders realized, because two-thirds of the fireplace construction is already in the walls forming the corner. Essentially only a third wall needs to be built to lean into that corner from floor to ceiling and above. If for any reason no corner of a particular room is suitable for a fireplace, a partial partition wall of adobe may be constructed to provide a corner somewhere else in the room as shown in the above illustration. (For preliminary study in the use of adobe, see pages 30-36 in *Adobe Architecture.*)

"A simple adobe" is a commonly heard comment about an adobe

house. It gratefully acknowledges an escape from complexity of materials and labor — from complexity in general. This simplicity came about naturally in the early history of the use of adobe as a building material. A man's land and his house material were one, and his labor his own. His skill in masonry — and the use of native timbers — was inherited from his fathers.

With a variety of materials becoming available and the hiring of labor appearing as the usual procedure an adulteration of the "adobe" took place. The outside walls were built thinner and inside walls were built of frame to cut down on the time and cost of labor.

In designing a house or choosing a corner for a fireplace in a house that is already constructed it would be well to think about why an all-adobe corner is ideal for an adobe fireplace. First, an adobe fireplace originated in an adobe corner; aesthetically this is what we relate to and try to emulate. Secondly it causes less apprehension as to being a fire hazard. Thirdly, an all-adobe corner constitutes a homogeneous mass which is the qualitative feature for even absorption, retention and radiation of heat, thus it is an energy conservation measure which, I would like to point out, calls for reassessment of the economic value of adobe walls in general.

My main concern is that you be aware that since adobe absorbs heat it will also conduct heat inward to the wall and that you take precaution if you are building against one or more stud walls. Though it is now claimed that adobe is fifteen to twenty-five percent better in insulating capacity than formerly believed, mass is the main feature in the holding of this quality. The precaution to insulate by an adequate number of inches of adobe or by some other means not only applies to the firebox area but to the chimney area in regard to the

proximity of stud partition, ceiling, viga and floors of wood.

I have used Wilfred Stedman's drawing (page 37) to illustrate the solution to two things. First, how a viga which may be in the way of building the fireplace flue and chimney can be cut back, at the time in construction that it becomes apparent it need be, to be flush with the face of the chimney. Before cutting it back, however, a lintel having places for its ends to rest securely into the corner walls, should be placed flush against the new chimney and under the viga to carry its weight. Neither the viga nor the lintel should be a part of the chimney structure so as not to be a fire hazard. The plastering of the chimney can be finished up tight underneath and down from above the lintel to pull it all together. Secondly, the drawing can give you an idea of where to cut a floor and joists back if you are planning to build a fireplace in a room that already has a wooden floor. The floor and joists will have to be cut on the line the hearth will take. These joists will have to be supported again by a cross piece nailed to their cut and to the joists which remain supported. This cut-back is necessary so that a reinforced foundation can be poured in and onto the ground to carry the weight of the main body of the fireplace and so that a six inch concrete slab can be poured for the hearth. If the fireplace is to be in a second story room you should consult your local building code about the thickness of a reinforced slab for that and as to how far into the corner walls it should rest on cross metal angle bars, and as to what gauge metal these bars should be. This will vary with the size and weight of the planned fireplace and with other features of construction.

THE BEST TIME TO PLAN a fireplace is when planning the house. But even if this is not done, a fireplace should be built as though it were planned for in the beginning,

with an adequate foundation and so that the chimney will not cause a problem in design or construction. To heat a room properly, a fireplace should be designed in proportion to the room. But the smoke-proof factor is in the proportions of the fireplace itself and the chimney. The sketch on this page shows the various measurements to be taken into consideration. The size of the fireplace opening is the key factor in fireplace design; however, you can see also that this might be decided by the height of the chimney. Ordinarily for a single story adobe room a chimney wouldn't be over fiteen feet high so we say, neither the throat area nor the flue tile area should be less than $1/12$ the area of the opening. We recommend the building-in of a metal throat and poker type damper unit for ease of construction and accuracy of proportions (see page 4 of *Adobe Architecture*). Having the width and height of your proposed fireplace opening and the chimney height, a lumber company will be able to supply you with the right size damper and

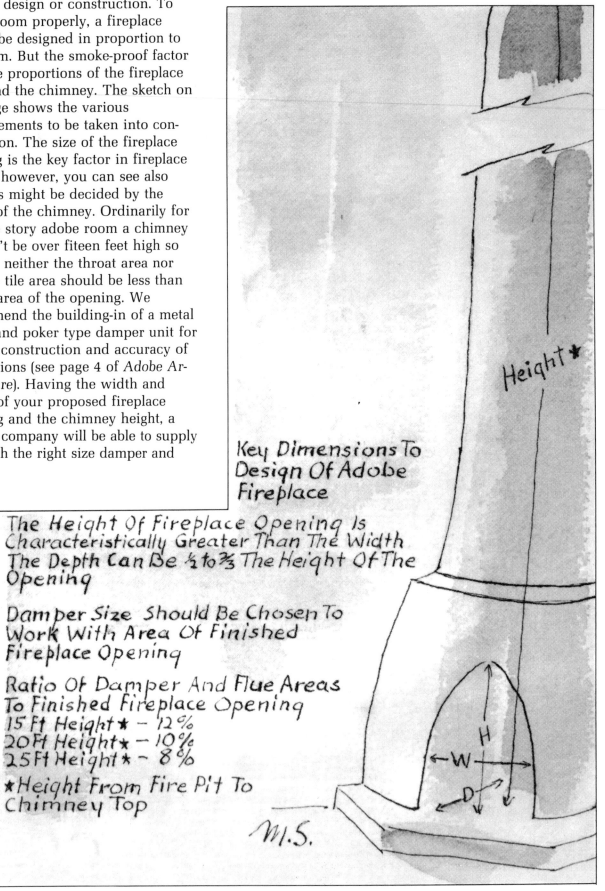

Key Dimensions To Design Of Adobe Fireplace

The Height Of Fireplace Opening Is Characteristically Greater Than The Width The Depth Can Be ½ to ⅔ The Height Of The Opening

Damper Size Should Be Chosen To Work With Area Of Finished Fireplace Opening

Ratio Of Damper And Flue Areas To Finished Fireplace Opening
15 Ft Height★ – 12%
20 Ft Height★ – 10%
25 Ft Height★ – 8%

★Height From Fire Pit To Chimney Top

M.S.

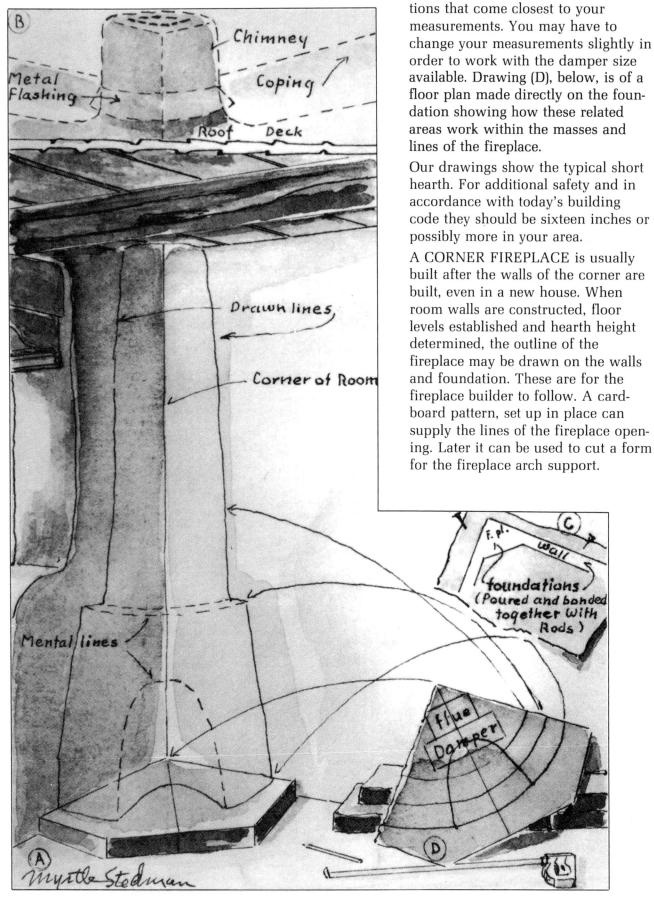

Chimney

Coping

Metal Flashing

Roof   Deck

Drawn lines,

Corner of Room

Mental lines

Mental lines

F. pl.

wall

foundations.
(Poured and bonded
together with
Rods )

flue

Damper

Myrtle Stedman

the right size and number of flue tiles from the manufacturer's specifications that come closest to your measurements. You may have to change your measurements slightly in order to work with the damper size available. Drawing (D), below, is of a floor plan made directly on the foundation showing how these related areas work within the masses and lines of the fireplace.

Our drawings show the typical short hearth. For additional safety and in accordance with today's building code they should be sixteen inches or possibly more in your area.

A CORNER FIREPLACE is usually built after the walls of the corner are built, even in a new house. When room walls are constructed, floor levels established and hearth height determined, the outline of the fireplace may be drawn on the walls and foundation. These are for the fireplace builder to follow. A cardboard pattern, set up in place can supply the lines of the fireplace opening. Later it can be used to cut a form for the fireplace arch support.

39

Floor plan (cut-out) for bed of adobe mortar

It would be well to have the flue tiles and metal damper handy so that you get a feeling for them before you actually have to build them in with the adobes. Standard size 10 x 14 inch adobes are used. Each adobe may have to be cut to fit the particular position it is to occupy. Many sound pieces left-over from the house building process may be used as a savings of material.

TO START THE ADOBE FIREPLACE, mud mortar is spread where it is needed on the foundation for the laying-up of the walls of the firebox, and the first two adobes are laid as in Drawing E. If the firebox is being built against one or more frame walls, Pattern F should be followed so that there will not be fewer than 10 inches of wall between the fire and inflammable material. If the fireplace is being built against adobe walls, the first five courses may gradually attain the shape of Pattern H, which will give a cradling shape to the back wall. (See also the cross-section in Drawing O).

Drawing I shows a plywood form for the building of the arch. It is cut one inch short and is set up on one inch wedges and has a prop hinged to its back. When the fireplace is com-

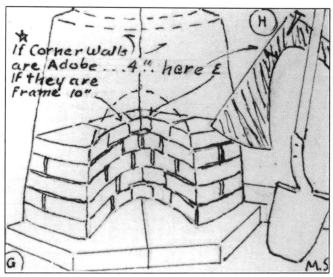

If Corner Walls are Adobe....4". here & If they are Frame 10"

Form for Arch

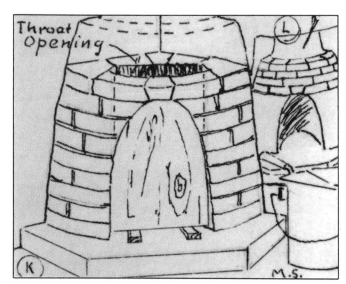

pleted, it can be let down and easily pulled forward and out. Drawing K shows this form doing its job.

ADOBES FOR THE ARCH are prepared by cutting them in half lengthwise. To cut adobe, score and tap the score with the edge of a trowel until the two halves separate. One end of the adobe is then shaped to fit against the form. A key is cut for locking the two sides of the firebox walls together. (See Drawings J, K and L).

INSIDE AND BEHIND THE ARCH, the side walls of the firebox would be built up parallel with the straight part of the opening. These side walls should be bonded with the back wall in such a manner that the back comes forward and up without corners until reaching the course which is to seat the metal throat and damper. Then this course should finish with a long rectangular opening the right size for this seating. The flat plane in back will be the baffle shelf. (See Drawings K and O).

Angle iron is used to get a square, or as shown in Drawings M and N, a rectangular opening. The iron is used as a lintel to carry adobes across the face of the fireplace. A layer of rock wool placed under its ends and in the

41

angle will prevent the cracking of the adobe.

Two courses carried across the angle iron and to the back should finish off with a baffle shelf and the rectangular opening for the throat and damper unit as mentioned above.

WHEN THE DAMPER UNIT IS IN PLACE, one-half inch of adobe mortar should be laid on the baffle shelf. This unit should also be built in at the ends and over the face closely enough to keep it from moving when the damper lever is operated, but not tight enough to crush the rock wool.

Fill in the corner, square the back and complete the walls of the smoke chamber following the dotted lines in Drawing P and following the cross-section Drawing O. If crushed paper is placed behind the damper when it is in an open position, it will keep the baffle shelf free of debris.

BRICKLAYER'S MORTAR such as Redimix or Richmortar can be used to join the flue tiles. Wrap the tiles with rock wool and encase with half adobes and adobe pieces. To secure the masonry, use strips of metal lath at intervals between courses with the ends of the lath nailed to the walls.

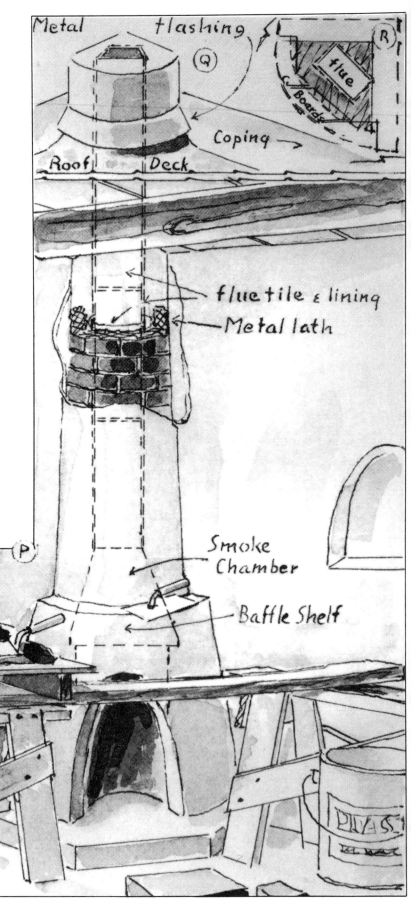

The ends of the ceiling boards that rest an inch or so on the chimney wall should be kept back four inches from the flue tile and have the protection of a fireproof material such as Vermiculite. At least two courses of the adobe chimney should be built up over the ends of the ceiling boards, the roofing material brought up and over them before the chimney is continued to a finish.

BEFORE THE FIREPLACE CAN BE PLASTERED and painted, it should be worked with a dull hatchet to sculpt the surfaces smooth of protrusions. The first coat of plastering should also be done with the idea of sculpturing the lines.

The rough coat and the finish coat of plastering should be done in the same manner and material as the walls that the fireplace is built against, finishing four inches inside the firebox area. (See Drawing P). The firebox area itself is best plastered only with adobe and straw, then a fine coat of mud plaster without straw but enough sand to get a smooth, uncracked surface.

The type of plastering so time-honored in adobe houses is done without affectation. It is smooth, but not too smooth, with an undulating softness that is lovely in flickering light.

A fireplace is for all seasons. May one be a place for many hours of happy fellowship, good conversation and peaceful meditation in your home.

# BIBLIOGRAPHY

*Adobe, Past and Present.* Santa Fe, NM: Museum of New Mexico Press, 1972.

Aller, Paul and Aller, Doris. *Build Your Own Adobe.* Stanford, CA: Stanford University Press, 1946.

Boudreau, Eugene H. *Making The Adobe Brick.* Berkeley, CA: Fifth Street Press, 1971.

Bunting, Bainbridge. *Early Architecture in New Mexico.* Albuquerque: University of New Mexico, 1976.

_____. *Of Earth and Timbers Made.* Albuquerque: University of New Mexico, 1974.

Chapman, Kate. *Adobe Notes.* Spanish Colonial Arts Society, 1966.

Gray, Virginia. *Mud Space & Spirit: Handmade Adobes.* Santa Barbara, CA: Capra Press, 1976.

Groben, W. Ellis. *Adobe Architecture: Its Design and Construction.* Seattle, WA: Shorey Bookstore, 1975.

Iowa, Jerome. *Ageless Adobe: History and Preservation in Southwestern Architecture.* Santa Fe, NM: Sunstone Press, 1985.

Lumpkins, William. Adobe Past and Present. Santa Fe, NM: Museum of New Mexico, 1972.

_____. *La Casa Adobe.* Santa Fe, NM: Ancient City Press, 1961.

McHenry, Paul G. *Adobe & Rammed Earth Buildings: Design & Construction.* Wiley, 1984.

_____. *Adobe: Build it Yourself.* Tucson: University of Arizona Press, 1985.

O'Connor, John F. *The Adobe Book.* Santa Fe, NM: Ancient City Press, 1973.

Scully, Vincent. *Pueblo Architecture of the Southwest.* Fort Worth: University of Texas, 1971.

Southwick, Marcia. *Build With Adobe.* Denver: Sage Books, 1966.

Stedman, Myrtle and Stedman, Wilfred. *Adobe Architecture.* Rev. ed. Santa Fe, NM: Sunstone Press, 1978.

# INDEX

Bonding: 10

Doors and doorways: 31-33
Dovetailing: 10

Electrical work: 11

Fireplaces
  Building: 40-43
  Corner: 39-40
  Dimensions: 38
  Planning and design: 36, 38-39
  Plastering: 43
  Restoration of: 22
Floors: 26-29
Foundations: 10, 24-25

Heating systems: 11
House plans: 8-9, 18-21, 30

New construction: 10

Paint: 16
Planning and design: 36, 38-39
Plaster, Adobe: 14-16, 43
Plaster, Hard: 16

Roofs: 11, 21-24
Ruins, Restoration of: 22-25

Vigas: 12-13

Walls: 10 12-14, 17-21, 24
Windows: 12, 30-31

# Myrtle Stedman

Myrtle Stedman was born in Charleston, Illinois. She grew up in the vicinity of Houston, Texas. As a child she was in close association with her designer-builder father, E.B. Kelly. She was personally acquainted, from planning stage to finish, with the building of pioneer homes, school and church which he worked on for the South End Land Company on the Westmoreland Farms and its accompanying town-site, Bellaire.

Myrtle's academic training started in 1927 when she was a student in the Houston Museum of Fine Arts

School. The Faculty was made up of instructors of painting and architecture from the Rice Institute, which has one of the highest standards for colleges in the United States. Later she entered the Stedman Studio on a life-time partnership basis and became engaged in practical experiences that could not be equaled by years of training in the usual manner. Her English born husband, Wilfred Stedman, whose background was in architecture as well as in painting and illustrating was recognized as one of the most outstanding artists of the Southwest. Because of their combined talents their studio was often involved in advertising artwork relating to the civic development of Houston. She and her husband were charter members of the Houston Artists Association and Myrtle became one of Houston's leading watercolorists.

Adobe architecture in New Mexico was one of Wilfred's favorite topics of conversation and Myrtle was instilled with the love of adobes before she ever saw one. In the early twenties Wilfred was sorely tempted to join artist friends who were building adobe studios and homes in Santa Fe but it wasn't until 1932 that a painting trip into the area resulted in the purchase of a productive fruit ranch, an old nursery and three existing adobe houses. One of the adobes was already over three hundred years old. Over a period of years they remodeled these and built others to supplement their income as artists and illustrators. Wilfred wrote a little book called *Santa Fe Homes, Charming and Practical*, and worked for Kruger and Clark Associated Architects on W.P.A. proposal presentations for schools, hospitals and public buildings to be built throughout the state of New Mexico. He also did the artwork and layout for a book called *New Mexico Home Plan Book* published by the *New Mexico Magazine*. All this time, Myrtle was gaining experience as construction foreman on home projects. There were many hours spent together in the studio with Myrtle helping her husband from time to time doing illustrations for the *New Mexico Magazine* or with pictorial maps and publications for the State Tourist Bureau. Always in the back of her mind was an adobe house.

After her husband's death in 1950 she became known as "Artist in Adobe" designing, building, and remodeling adobe homes under a contractor's license. These homes and the ones she owns and maintains on their acreage in Tesuque display a deep knowledge and authenticity in traditional construction. This is conveyed in *Adobe Architecture* by Myrtle and Wilfred Stedman, and now in *Adobe: Remodeling and Fireplaces.*

Myrtle's work in adobe or her books on adobe have been featured in the *New Mexico Magazine*; the *New Mexico Home Plan Book* (second edition); *Harper's Magazine*; the *Whole Earth Epilog*, and the *Santa Fean*. One of her houses was on a Denver Art Museum Tour and Myrtle gave a talk to the group on adobe.

She served for five years as a representative from her community at the Pojoaque Watershed District Board meetings; twelve years as a member of the Santa Fe County Advisory Council; and two years as a Board Member of Las Tres Villas when they were successful in keeping the Tesuque School from being closed. She and her husband were early members of the Old Santa Fe Association. She is a member of the San Gabriel Historical Society; the Colonial New Mexico Historical Foundation; the St. Vincent Hospital Auxiliary; of St. John's Library Association; and is classified as an "angel" Guild member of the Santa Fe Opera. She continues to paint and she walks her dog and cat in the old apple orchard.